IMPERFECT METAMORPHOSIS

Echoes of the Uncalm Mind

ISHAAN NAG

ISBN 979-8-88849-094-5

Contents

Indoctrinate

A habit of heinous rulers, filled to the brim,

With intolerance, cowardice, with tyrannical whims,

Too weak to accept the fact that contradictions exist,

Too weak to fight, too incompetent to convince,
too weak to resist.

Too weak to resist diabolic thoughts invading their mind,

Too evil to spread harmony, the thread which all of us
bind.

Everyone has the liberty to strive and adore an ideal,

The right to campaign, to convince, but in contact with
what is moral and real.

But when you are rendered weak by those ideas, and others
you now hate,

You lay your own grave against tyranny, a betrayal by fate,

A mind too narrow, too disabled to even tolerate,

The curse on free nations and people, the urge to
indoctrinate.

Storm

Burdened by humid creations of the universe,

Welcomed by those teeny-tiny parasites down below,

Unwelcome refugees, however, to this innocent turf,

He no longer wants to hunch and bow.

He no longer wishes to entertain, the pathetic beings below,

He no longer wants to be burdened by useless, sorrowed thoughts,

He no longer wants to sob in parasitic woe,

He no longer cares for the little ones, the poor, and the ones ailing in their cots.

He thinks that this is enough, the very drops which nourished the poor Earth down,

The favour not appreciated, immorality never abating, will now be redemption,

A quiet rumble, preceding the gleeful, sadistic, liberated howl,

Then starts the storm, to return to it's past joy, glory, without a care for their verdict, assumption

The Rude Customer

He comes into the world, on a fateful invite,

In the whole debacle, he causes chaos and fights,

He throws other innocent customers out of their revel,

He ruins, this horrendous customer, violates values who others hail.

He challenges the saintly customer who wants to improve this great ball,

His mind is too narrow to revel and let revel, he puts up a wall,

For he markets his own heinous ideas of hate, to judge customers on what they wear,

Instead of their choices, their soul, the ones which matter, only animosity this cult does share.

When all the customers could hand in hand, coexist with dignity,

Without groups, us and they, oppressors and oppressed, what a pity.

A sigh, even though the damage is done, when it is their time to leave,

It offers comfort, no compatriot, a burden left in the form of The Rude Customer, a sigh of relief.

Dust Devil

All foundations are shaken, when it comes to play,
To unfortunate revelations of incompetence, it gives way,
We realize how weak we are, how weak towards change,
How easily our joy and peace can be destroyed,
this is a revenge.

A revenge towards stubborn resistance to contradictions,
Revenge towards false shows of strength, which is only
fiction.
But if strong enough, the dust will not clash, but embrace,
If you are flexible, if you are rational and string, that must
be the case.

The dust devil will feel your weakness, your strength,
your fear,
The dust devil will either bless your world with breeze,
or let it tear.
The dust devil wins when fools divide themselves,
The dust devil blesses the united and strong, those not
scared, if need be, to delve.

My Utopia

Minds drift back, to a wonderland of comfort,

Carved out of resplendent tapestries, infiltrate sounds
of a concert,

Beneath is an ocean of joy and freedom, which is acid
to sorrowful thoughts,

Rivers drift calmly, supplying nectar of euphoria forever,
to a land without a drought.

Riding on Pegasus, breeze embracing, fairies sing of
accepting all,

Regardless of aspects people cannot change, virtue rightly
rewarded in the hall,

Where true, moral justice is served, where all get what
they deserve,

Where ideas are freely discussed and heard, contradicted,
no one, nothing is reserved.

A place where clouds of tolerance and openness,
clash to provide drops,

Of ideas, of opinions, though none bigoted, for hate
is already mopped,

But all contradicting, all fearless, none polluted and
censored,

Will be my, admittedly hypocritical Utopia, a place
of eternal unity and mirth.

The First

I had skipped queues without deserving to, shocked looks
I had received,

I had played with the balance of trust, in other words,
I had deceived,

I had signalled a hug, but instead packed a punch,

I had signalled to jump, but instead I hunched.

I had snatched opportunities, from people who needed so,

I had turned deaf to cries of agony and woe,

Only so I could save some moments, I turned away
precious chances,

To be moral, to be human, but cruel vanity dances.

After sinking hopes, chances, and trust,

On to the finish line, myself I had thrust.

Yet at what cost, had I gained the flaunting rights,
without any mirth,

Shying away from humanity and justice, I had
unfortunately become first.

The Drips

The tap was turned off for sure, but the melody could
be heard,

Soft, teasing melodies of incompetency, muting the
whistling bird,

Resounding in the reaches of our soul, melodies of
frustration and regret,

Resounds the slow drips, almost instilling hate.

The drips of acid, of salty disappointment, when you fail
the world,

You hope to let it gush, or even let it be closed,

But the slow, delicate drips pierce the very essence,

Of our souls, minds and hearts, reminding us about
individual pains.

The drips, also hopeless, saying that is all that is left,

Of water, of kindness, of morals, most lost in theft,

By situations, and savage mindsets, who nearly
turned off the tap,

The drips serving as a constant reminder of what
we abundantly could have.

Lethargic to Changes

Why do minds and habits cease to change, and when they really do,

Why do they steady with lethargic tantrums, and resisting change too,

Why does inertia take fancy upon these reserved emotions,

Why can't you change? Why can't you for once be then filled with elation?

Or rather, they are not emotions, but involuntary actions,

Never wanting to abate it's rather inconvenient traction,

Holding on to behaviour which we wish it did not,

No surprise, for it to be more flexible we all have sought.

Clichéd jokes about failed resolutions are probably true,

But these habits and mentalities, let us at least try to sue.

Let us energize these lethargic tantrums, when we want it shall abate,

Let us make it flexible, before it's too late.

At the End

I don't know what lies at the end,

A new road, adventurous moods to try new trends,

Maybe an alley which seems right,

Not appealing to logic, but pulls at the conscience
with might.

But at the end there might be sorrow, after a journey
through our ideal land,

There might be nostalgia for that meadow, as we enter
a country of sand,

There might also be joy as we feed on the bounty we collect,

From the playground of all beings peaceful and living,
and the ecstasy we recollect.

There might be more joy, as the snippets of the wonderful
place and time,

Into our mind, our heart, and emotions, a way do find.

In any case, I don't know what it is at the end,

So I might as well enjoy this mud path, be readily anxious
at the ends.

The Last Screech

Maybe it's a signal of frustration with the present,

Maybe a signal against a dystopian future if the rod is
further bent,

The rod used to push motives and desires, and also,
of course luck,

But when we fail to see that it's impossible, we bend,
it bursts, our desires into the muck.

Maybe the screech is a final stand against the injustice we
have done,

To everything, living, non living, metaphysical, fooling you
into thinking you won,

But in fact it was the preparation for their last stand,

To exterminate your joyful or miserable existence, all that
was required was a swap of the hand.

So yes, the screech, be it from your scorned but correct
mother, or your fate,

Is but a warning gesture, warning you to abate,

Just as the howls Bernard heard before he was shoved,

Into the great destroyer of tyrannical voices, the blade that
was so loved.

Often stigmatized as something mundane,

Only for sane people, or maybe, a little too sane,

For people who are bland, who resist spice in life,

Shuns for this activity is very rife

While that is true to some extent, there is some beauty
to that,

A kind of monotonous, inoffensive charm, a kind of
repetitive pat,

A kind of certainty, a lack of risk which a few do enjoy,

No unpredictable disaster, no "land ahoy ".

Maybe our kind is bland, but that is but prejudice,

Maybe we are wary of unknown waves in unknown seas,

But that does not make us bland, for inside us might hide,

Stories and lectures sure to capture in a trance, and shiver
everyone's hide.

A Melancholic End

Why does it feel so wretched, after eyes are revealed,

As the fantasy is left behind, as the bag of dreams are sealed?

Why does even good news, seem irrelevant,

Why do we, unfairly, on people who don't deserve,
our irritation vent?

As we emerge from the woolly cocoon, we certainly
don't evolve,

Into the cheerful spirit of a butterfly, yet melancholic
mysteries we do solve,

Mysteries full of tragedy, yet none have, do,
or will ever affect,

Our life, our people, or any other aspect.

Yet, though not all, quite a few,

Go through this damaging, shattering slew

Of attacks and wars on our emotional foundation,
when fate lends

A helping hand to the belligerent, which, to a "refreshing"
rest, causes a melancholic end.

The Moral Dictatorship

There remains standing an invisible book of rules,

Serving to make us Homo sapiens be tools,

And slaves of peace and love, and be wholesome,

Dictated by the majority, and their violation is done
by some.

But I'm a slave too of this constitution, so shall everyone be,

To protect everyone from unnecessary horror, and loss
of dignity,

To protect everyone from ending their life, the greatest
gift they could receive,

The clay which they could bend to their will,
giving them relief.

A master which works hard to tame the disgusting hate,

Against fellow beings, based on aspects they can't change,
though growing wilder as of late.

But rejoice, all fellow followers, for we outnumber,

The enemies of this dictatorship, though many of the
soldiers are going into slumber.

Honourable Flee

There are only so many jeers and stones that can be
endured,

There can only be so many faces you can see,
with intentions impure,

There can only be so much lenience towards unjustified
intolerance,

When morality and basic dignity is banished towards you,
prevails then no sense.

Then fly, my poor, but now brave victim, and try to peck
out their malice,

Fly, my shunned and stigmatised bird, bite and dodge,
don't let it cease,

Don't let it cease until their poison is thrown,

Or don't let it stop until the battle against this burden
is won.

Fly, my newly-freed bird, free of insults and torture,

Fly, to carve out a new life for you, your new ideas you
nurture,

Just like the kids you could have fed, Peace and Harmony,

Both martyred, fighting bravely against diabolic tyranny.

My bird, your feathers are strewn with red, some fallen off,

Fallen protection, bravado, revealing the fragile body, the tragedy of loss.

Fly away and carve out a life of dignity, solace, over the fields of heather,

Fly away, their bird, steady your quivering feathers.

The Same Old

Everyday seems like a video on loop,

A day in motion, but imprisoned in a coop,

A coop of repetition, exasperation, not necessarily bored,

But it seems the same throughout, the same old.

The same old suffering, the same old misery,

The same old patterns, yet unpredictable, marred with treachery.

The same old embrace by the wind and the loved,

The same old luxury, the same old privilege of getting what is deserved.

The same old emotions, the same old sensations,

The same old lack of extreme pain, and elation.

The same old days are now yearned, once to the world we have sold,

The same old salty tears yearn for that same old company, the same old, same old.

Crack

They fall, those bones, with a short call,

Struggling to manage that precious ball,

Just like sudden hopes, and shattering disappointment,

The wound can be healed, but the scarred pride shuns
every ointment.

It stabs, stabs into the valued thing,

That hard, simple block, hiding the riches of the king,

Or maybe the spirit of the room, wailing for us to return,

But first, we must stab the vexed hole, and then turn.

The knife, though, must be the right one too,

The wails must be suppressed; the mouth must be sewed,

Else the true identity will want to be free,
and the tolerance to submit will lack,

Nothing will be shrouded in mist, nothing will be
concealed, neither shrieks of joy, nor the crack.

Start

Some of us like to hunch and peer to the front,

Arms in a zigzag, and the eyes on a hunt,

For the best route, the shortest contour,

Only the finishing line, them lure.

But some of us prefer to linger, and get to know,

Turn competitors to companions, together through
the high, low,

Some of us like to set our eyes, onto the luscious
cherry trees,

Some of us like to achieve, but not just the finish line, and
also appreciate the flowers and bees.

Some of us like to meander away, and don't care if we
come last,

Some of us follow our mind, but heart too, and don't care if
trouble strikes sudden, fast.

Some of us like to be irrelevant but happy, some of us want
to play a part,

Some of us have goals more than just finishing, or no goals
at all, but either way, we must start.

Coup

It had duties to attend to, important ones,

It had to see which solutions work, and ensure that they run,

Obligated by a workload necessary for governance,

But all of that was discontinued, what happened hence.

Later, the elected mind was replaced with a distracting coup,

Sombre officials were captured, rendering them redundant, and nothing they could do,

For they knew, that what the nation, the boy needed, was them, and that he knew,

But the droll coup was what he wanted, and involuntary support wasn't few.

All that interrupted the parties and the playtime, the sunny picnics were quakes,

Barely felt, barely meant, but mere moral shakes,

By the weak army in the head loyal to the elected mind,

But nothing it could do to displace and continue the duties, no reinforcement could it find.

Wheels

I hope from the bottom of my heart, for the sake of those spikes,

May they spin, may they continue to shove aside pebbles as they traverse roads lined with pine,

Let them please just go on with that seem velocity,

Not lagging and then accelerating, and they won't thus cause animosity.

Let this not stop, let these determined wheels carry us away,

 Away from that nightmarish, expanding faults, engulfing the day,

The great big flow of red hot molten horror, eroding joy,

Let these once be looked back at, and faintly too, dismissed as a phase, making lives toys.

Let the wheels boldly, bravely, and most of all, proudly flee,

Let them flee, let them run, until the troubled past we can't see,

Let them run, let nothing else do, especially the mind, else the raging storm may kill,

The only saviour being the ever running, ever rotating, spiked wheels.

Pebbles on the Road

It is a miserable experience for many, to be dragged out
of the refuge,

Every little mistake seems a calamity, huge,

Every little event seems an earthquake,

As, from the warm, fluffy shelters in a freezing morning,
they make us wake.

Walking barefoot oftentimes, for reasons tyrannical,
or even unknown,

Every step seems like a punishment for an imaginary sin,
we atone,

Or maybe we are just blind enough to see,

The unnecessary injustice we caused, so thus the miserable
morning hours of wee.

An assignment, a cruel one, to collect the pebbles on the
road,

Representing all the obligations, enemies of the lethargic
soul,

Oftentimes some of us feel that we had rather be empty
and be bored,

Rather than, pick up pebbles on the road.

Leaf

As her companions abandon to escape the cold,

She stands without any of her beings, proud and bold,

Frail and dry, shrivelled, but with confidence and admiration,

For herself, and the nature, her home, but both are without
elation.

Both are ignored, both sullied, and their importance
neglected,

They think to themselves as they reminisce the past,
back when respected,

Back when their significance was understood,

Seems like they used to be enlightened, but now vision
covered with soot.

No one cares about the wind, and the liquid transparent
wonder,

No one cares about this green, fading leaf, as it gets blown
yonder,

Yet as she gets shoved aside, brushed aside, harassed,
she breathes her last,

For the sake of those very beings, who ignored her pain,
else they will leave too fast.

Review

Very ironic, it is, for sometimes that is all we seek,

But usually at a time when the ego does peak,

And positive ones are all we can tolerate,

Anything otherwise, is met with instant hate.

Sometimes, some of us genuinely are out to seek a truthful reply,

Negative, positive, all treated equal at face value, none will make them cry.

All they require is criticism, no matter how harsh, but it better be fair,

Yet with no guarantee, they are out to risk their pride, ego, into the dragon's lair.

But more often than not, it is not a review, only an excuse for hearing praises,

Like the same reward for everyone, even adults, no matter what the position in the races,

Yet all will be hypocritical, for even the author himself is guilty, and times not a few,

Let us all strive to hear reviews, when we ask for a review.

Cold

It penetrates deep, into the bones and thoughts,

Ice adorning landscapes, while makes merry the frost,

And some cry with misery, tears freezing into ice,

Increasing the anguish, the pain, of the anguished and
pained, nature never let's then thrive.

Yet the one with a smile on the face, initially forceful, true,

Does not bow down to the freeze, but tries to woo,

The ice, and embrace the cold, yet later it warms,

He makes merry, he prances in capers, inviting euphoria
in swarms.

Of course not the first aid it is, but it surely helps to put
a smile,

It helps find satisfaction in misery, which must be a pretty
good goal of life.

If not possible in all cases, but let's be bold,

Enough to plan for the worst and hope for the best,
as we face the cold

Liberty to Restrict

There he came by preaching freedom, yet he used to lash,

At anyone he used to disagree with, he was quite a rash,

Of irony in the face of what he ostensibly advocates,

For dissent, a significant lesson in his self-proclaimed aim, he violently hates.

He carries a hatchet, to enforce what he is feeling,

He carries a hammer to hammer nails into one's mind, or he sends them reeling,

When they beg to disagree, he muffles their weapon to declare,

What they think (or don't), but now too afraid to share.

He jeers and destroys the dignity of his policies' critics,

He smells disagreement, and with the excuse of securing liberty, he muffles, of hypocrisy he reeks.

And when confronted, he either jails, or he does digress,

Or if in a brave, strong, mood, he intends to say, "I have the liberty to oppress".

The Climb

Each pull of the hand filled with excruciating pain,

Reminding nightmares, barely sane,

Each pull is equated by a pull from beneath,

A reluctant yet strong, a despised but compelling urge,
to let the hell below sheath.

Open it's mouth, as he falls, and swallow him into eternal
ruin,

He knows, he hates, he wants to escape, but he is still
pulled by the sin.

He wants to escape, that's why he climbs,

But now, he barely prefers it to hell, as he sings hymns.

Barely motivated, he reaches a camp, and he is instilled,

With new found energy, new found confidence, and
virtuous feelings, distilled.

He now thinks he maybe can reach the peak, and the hell,
a memory he would rather forget,

But faint, flickering, and glad no longer and inferno,
he would be happy with what he would get.

Protected

Each winter morning, a privileged in a blanket,

Each warrior, thought without fear, wants to be protected, from hatchets,

Or cold, unwelcome winds and misty anonymity,

Hiding something hideous usually, yet still shrouded in ambiguity.

Now some feel protected from wholesome changes, using force,

Protected from letting their chances to exploit be taken away, and a source,

Of violence, of misleading and above all fear,

They feel protected for those few moments, until the swarm stampedes, the curtains tear.

I don't see what's wrong with feeling protected, if you can afford to feel,

I have no problem with this emotion, as long as we separate real from reel,

As long as you scurry with the first call to duty, to flee or to fight,

As long as you remember wearing an armour, doesn't make you a knight.

Prisoner

With chains made of Circumstances, I am told,

With bars of Prevention, reportedly my soul they want
it to be sold,

With teasing winds from outside extinguish the last,
faint breath,

Of what once used to be raging fire of liberty, reduced to
lingering smokes of death.

A house carved out of humility, locked in one's own home,

Constant pacing and unproductive fuming, we just want
to roam,

Yet really blinded and prisoner of our vision we are,

Temporary or prolonged freedom, losing vision of what we
hold more dear.

The chains might be made of situation, but the burn
is our folly,

The unnecessary fumes feeding on insecurity,
while we launch volleys,

A necessary temporary detention turned into
a self-made hell,

A prisoner in ship in a fatal mental storm, though the
rather short journey could be a smooth sail.

Get Well Soon

While maladies riddle us and hope seems lost,

When every tree feels naked and bare, all its leaves lost,

No matter how green and lush, every colour seems pale,

Cheer seems in high demand, is seemingly put to sale.

When one can do well to get rid of fancies they previously liked,

 Pain and sorrow and guilt accentuated, all of them hike.

It doesn't matter if miserable drops don't stop, or if the birds coo,

A frown is there, and justifiably, and tends to maintain too.

Though tough to do so, and I understand, I say let's just attempt,

To ignore the pain, and misery for once, and tidy our hair, unkempt.

Let's turn that frown upside down, and every day seems a boon,

Let's try, let's just try, and get well soon.

To Feel

To feel, to consciously notice that the thread over your skin,

Kisses each single cell of that live blanket, though as
you will have seen,

It's passion only visible, stuck in pretence,

For we seek quite unsuccessfully it's emotions,
unknown it is whence.

To feel, is to let the heart pain, and hate it vehemently,

To feel, is to have a bad conscience, be justly bothered, for
it is not saintly,

To the morals, and of course, to feel is to possess,

That abstract tug keeping you from being a thing, from
taking part in a diabolic race.

To feel is to pay attention to every breath, every smile,

To feel is to pay attention to every minute itch, the border
between each tile,

Sometimes, to really see and feel beyond the physical fence,

You have to be blind and numb, to really, feel, and sense.

Spring

Often stereotyped as disloyal, and unpredictable notions,

By the incompetent, impertinent and those who lack
a lotion,

For their unknown, involuntary, undetected jealousy,

For not being able to change with times, and taking
this as an insult, heresy.

Though only those who have had puny, and limited minds
of their own,

Have in their own, and the rest of innocent society,
the seeds of animosity sown,

And each slight plot twist offend these delicate creatures,

(I know the title was not what you thought about),
look what that does teach us.

It teaches, a little bit of flexibility is the need of the hour,

Quite literally too, to stay relevant and thrive,
though other's mood it might sour.

Hence some of us versatile but peaceful, who just want
to live and let live, the two wings,

Of peaceful survival, and we want to spice that same life,
and just function well, just like a spring!

Give me Back

As I handed over the present to my very own friend,

It felt like a tearful goodbye, I had rather lend,

Than give away my precious, which for moments I have
possessed,

A gift I myself am aware, that I won't use and go to waste.

Give me back those moments, when only euphoria ruled,

When reality only a branch of the ideal dream, morning
not greeting with drools,

But only those precious moments, and navigate,

Around the sorrowful, agitated, nightmarish, abrasive ones,
the ones where we were used as bait.

Give me back, but only those times I missed a chance,

To shine, to retaliate with a magnificent comeback,
and cut the chains with a lance,

Representing being bound by unfounded humility,
liberated with newfound wit,

Give me back those incidents I wax poetic about,
or let me achieve them bit by bit.

I have a Duty

I have a duty, of being wholesome and kind,

Though this feels like a preachy childish pledge, i wish we would find,

A sincere attraction in following these lines, to live and let live,

Create a habitat beneficial for us and them, without being filtered through a sieve.

A sieve of social "standards" with parameters too ludicrous to exist,

Judging based on something they can't change, and they mustn't, and we insist,

To "fit", to "act" and mould oneself,

Into an illusion, and be shrouded in a miserable fake cloud, which makes the others feel safe.

I have a duty to possess such morals, and to provide for loved ones and me,

To do so by fair means, and not ridicule the ones with possession wee,

It is fine to decide not to donate, but at least have the urge,

I have a duty to enjoy an aimless life as well, not paying attention to jumps and the lurch.

Missed

Each step feels too slow, not swift enough,

Each stone too merciless, each terrain too rough,

Yet never bothering to pick sides, standing on the
confluence,

And never bothering to look around, to be overwhelmed
and influenced.

Standing on the pedestal between the plain and mountain,

Between sand and the sea, a potential delight turned
into pain,

Missing people in need, company, sanity, and chances,

To escape from this bland, artificial debacle, not knowing
what is, and how one dances.

Missing the very essence of whatever we received,

After each of us emerged from our own mothers,
for we sometimes deceive,

And confuse, necessary activities with our purpose,
making it unwanted strife

Even though the limbs and conscience pains, we miss,
the very essence of life

Dear Diary

Dear diary, every day of my life gets tattooed into
your pages,

Dear diary, as each allied day greeted and others war wages,

Sometimes you become the sweet journal of poems,
and sometimes a punching bag,

The physical mark, the contours on you all worth it,
for behind you never lag.

Forever updated on my life, a stalker I'm willing to confide,

A stalker without eyes and expressions but eternal
curiosity, a stalker who I let reside,

On my desk, in my house, my conscience, as that inky
fragrance,

Lures the laziest of hands, most misty of emotions
to take refuge, imprinting all feels and sense.

Dear diary, sometimes I feel, is my essence worth only
some delicate, flexible, rectangles?

When an emotional escape comes to mind, a group
of pages in the mind jangles?

But then I realize, you are the special one, worthy to catch
our worth,

The only refuge which gladly accepts refugees, dear diary,
waiting even when aeons, covered in dirt.

The Last Pedestal

Swept by winds of deadlines, whooshing and ticking away,

Yet the hardy harness anchors well on the rocks of
knowledge, opinions, gathered over days,

Yet seem like millennia, and stable symbiosis maintains
itself,

The harness full of dexterity and the right amount of
confidence, keeping the climber fully safe.

Yet the winds grow stronger, and the lack of pedestals
don't matter any more,

The meteoric rise seems to gradually cease, no more
can we soar,

Only two steps left to reach the top, and we don't mind
the cold,

So much preparation, ages of formation, we have been
rightly bold.

A certainty to conquer the only pedestal standing
in the way,

More the conviction of the wind to sweep us away.

Not a single rock or stone between the pedestal and
the top,

And as we reach, we slip and are swept, scowling at
the last pedestal, all inflated hopes are popped

Janus

That face with not a single blemish,

Striking eyes yet innocent, frank words all discomfort makes vanish,

Yet hiding under that naïve face lies a scheming weasel,

Wide eyes encompassing persona, flattery, on humbleness does chisel.

Hiding under a harmonious present lies a horrid past,

Which it wants to bury further, and make it cease to last.

Yet that intention is the most noble, while a faction hides,

Which yearns for the Devil to show, for the shrieks during genocide.

Under a brutal, vengeful face lies a country of light,

The real intention of that rugged jaw, war it wants to fight.

The same expressions we chuckled at, now seem to horrify,

Janus, you don't hide, one from the other, but both from both, just don't simplify.

The Plougher

She takes her shovel and digs all day,

Deep and deep, until she finds the crimes we did lay,

No matter how minute, she spots the dullest shine,

She crosses all layers, in her hunt, she crosses each line.

She ploughs for each inconsequential blunder,

Each ineffective flaw she hunts, the criminal's peace
of mind she plunders.

Oftentimes she doesn't need to dig, just conjure,

And masking a smile with a cross frown, and mentally
torture and injure.

Maybe she wants to improve her subjects, but one thing
she really hides,

A strange, faint but sadistic urge, which comes in waves
and tides,

She can't help it, but there is no denying, she likes that
heave-ho,

She, for once, doesn't mind the tracing sweat,
she craves the plough.

I Can

I can murder you and feed on your sorrow,

I can make and carve a hell out of every tomorrow,

And snatch your rightful and use it to enrich my own
pockets,

Strangle and snatch and scar your throat, as I steal
your gold locket.

I can be materially rich, but socially ostracized,

I can tolerate revolts, and perform genocides,

But then I will be left alone, and against everyone else,
I can only cave,

Or be left alone, again, with abundance of scarcity,
no one left to save.

I can fight against the "cowardly" world, whose morals
left intact,

I, however, would be in trouble if they lose that, and then
relentlessly attack.

The lack in me was my strength, has become weakness
again, never reflecting moments rude,

I invested too much on whether "I" can, not whether
I should.

If I Were You

Each crime would be justified, and with good reasons at that,

Each murder seems well deserved, magnifying a matter
so tad,

Each late wake-up appeals, and is met with sympathy,

And you would think I'm going against all forms of empathy.

And you should too, is what you think, but you
misunderstand,

I say, immoral crimes should shame the perpetrators,
and they want a hand,

To show them the spiritual way out, before a slap,

By that very hand, and if we can tap,

Into their souls, then we too feel no pity,

But do feel so when nature, or fellow beings unfairly act,
and it's usually not so pretty.

And not even pity, but we would feel for once, how
disaster causes pain,

And not load our burdening anger, instead we must tame,

And if this be the real world, then I say the difference
between heaven and earth is few,

Except maybe the time or call, but I would not sweat it,
if I were you.

Downpour

As the weather cries and sorrows, it is usually mirrored,

By the mortals below, and send them running away,
dear thunder feared,

And channel the wrath the land-dwellers caused, from
their pathetic cities,

Scratching at your body, for decades, though admirable
their queer abilities.

And also their queer belief that it's ego is unjustified,

Their belief that some will be spared, only to themselves,
they lied.

Yet that wrath finds a reflection, against unfairness,
lack, and personal strife,

Maybe hypocritical, but scorning at the judgemental
assumptions, which seem rife.

 And then comes a day when the poker face erodes,

The acid escapes and celebrates, the narrow vote.

It might look ugly, but it is the most beautiful liberation,
and let the agony soar,

And display to own self, the visibly horrible but
intrinsically charming, acidic, downpour.

Chant

The continuous, often vague sounds, but catching our unconscious attention,

There's many for each situation, joy, death, or tension,

And even though they sound gibberish, they sure make themselves known,

What a queer wonder, an earworm often sown.

The one of few kinds which often unite,

The cause is recalled, and a strange fire inside ignites.

A fire on which the sword of purpose can be moulded very well,

All thanks to the chant, stories of their noble cause which tells.

Even the most inhumane of aims are marketed as the best,

"Because of this certain group, my country goes to waste",

No matter how inconsiderate and naïve, we shout and pant,

And often sway everyone else, through the chant.

Willing Pain

Yes the wish is fulfilled, you are free to go,

Away from those searing hot chains of woe,

Away from disability, to perform and enjoy life,

Yet as the day resembles the past, why miss the strife?

Why prefer to be warmed by torture instead of lush blankets?

Why prefer the company of sorrow instead of the mates?

Why be so ungrateful to the liberty you craved?

Why not be thankful that you are saved?

Oh, you miss the cold relief, and the balm of each rare break,

In those breaks of euphoria, solace you did take.

But please be free from this sensation, it's just the cunning chains calling, let it be in vain,

This is just manipulation, no "willing pain. ".

Watermelon

Bite into this fleshy, red, moist being, and the water gushes out,

A brittle state of mind, much miserable than a mere pout,

The seeds being the last, delicate guards against hostile teeth,

Sunny memories rudely deemed redundant, with no authority to even visibly seethe.

Such gushing liquid gulped with utter gusto and pleasure,

Uninvited, burdening, even falsely miserable concerns, prizing such tears, like treasure,

A pity the peel is taken off,

A pity the rational mind stripped off for unjustified tensions, attracting only scoffs.

Pity such a protective, prized peel, for granted has been taken,

Pity, the knowledge that friendly company is a medicine, is forsaken.

Yet fortunate are we, for we can possibly get rid of such venom,

Yet it can't fend off such hostile, sharp, prying teeth, though I mustn't, I say, poor watermelon.

The Same

What a world, where half lives in darkness,

While the other half basks in sunny blessings, though foolishness,

Would be to assume that these are eternal,

And again, what a wonder, they alternate, between divine and infernal.

And what a wonder, that the fellow person sitting next to you, has a different opinion,

Associating completely different values, to those two, one is the scion

Of freedom and spreading fraternity, and loving all,

While one is brought as an unwanted judge, trying to convince otherwise is like talking to a wall.

What a wonder, where just a mountain or a coil,

Separates two bitter rivals, and human longing does foil.

What a wonder, the same world contains the wise and fools, one clearly the superior,

The same person changes own message and what it apparently prizes, the same mind, interior.

Stretch

Cracking knuckles, cracking thunder, cracking institutions,
Bellows of change, or at least it's promise, is the solution,
To the worn out and tired status quo,
For a restless new one, with a real life, we pledge
to say less no.

Yet which "one" are we talking about, how vague
can we be?
We mean buildings, bodies, passion and thoughts,
we pledge to see,
More, beyond the cloud of what we only wish to spot,
We pledge to not be cruel, and leave the old to rot.

We pledge to yawn and release the burden of our soul,
And pledge to oil our resourcefulness, and play
a bigger role,
Though small anyways, in the great framework
of material life,
Let's rush forward, oh no, I'm too drowsy, let's just leave
this pointless strife.

Side Pillow

My saviour from fragile nights, always by my side,

Ready to bear the brunt of heavy bodies and hearts,
not minding that we don't realize,

The value, the prizes they deserve, to bear infinite tears,

To bear scars and pain from wielding them in anger
and ecstasy, yet there is no fear.

Of them leaving, in times most needed or not,

They will always be there, never forgetting,
though we might let them rot.

Yet such side pillows exist, just much better,

They will understand and sympathize, but of weakness
they are a hater,

Something which they solve through love, or if in someone
else, through harsh words of reality,

To self respect and loyalty both, they pledge fealty.

They also don't think themselves inferior, for they are not,

While inanimate pillows don't mind it, if you forever forgot,

Their value, and the moral debt you owe,

What a joy to have someone so close, though more than
just a side pillow!

Shame

Always haunting the bravery of the decorated,

Always bravely challenging the cruelty of the immoral,
and the rightly hated,

What an utopia, if those who deserved you, were invaded,

By you, and those who didn't, wish they bravely waded.

Bravely waded across the murky waters of expectations,

And possess the strength to not be taken down by
desertion,

Of hopes to ask and be granted a favour,

Bravely wade to advocate justice for all, to be a saviour.

But is shame himself enough to decide whom he must
possess?

Is shame enough to stop the evil, and the worthy raise,

High enough, to obtain deserved fame?

If only I could find out, what a shame!

Alone

No prying eyes looking for discipline in the gaits of the walk,

The walk to eternal freedom, a toast to liberty, and there
are no hawks,

To supervise and judge, and give scathing remarks,

Or flatter, for that matter, ignore the barks.

No moral obligation to even hear, let alone listen,

To demands in the form of mere suggestions, nor any reason,

To attend to calls for manners and diet which suit in their
eyes and mind,

To be flustered by their rebukes, or even try to hide.

No sweat dropping for, there is no one to review,

How one conducts oneself, no need to sigh a "phew",

In relief when the moment passes, and as you wait for the
flight,

Your flight abroad, to adulthood, and it's first sight.

And you swear, swear to not be commanded,

You swear to brush rebukes off, when you are reprimanded.

And with such a thought of freedom, you feel you won.

As you lean to the side, as you wait for the flight, welcomed
by absence, you are alone.

Whistle

What an expert in hiding the stew of emotions
cooking inside,

Brimming with humid tears, yet suppressing that tide,

An urge to blow the whistle, yet you bite the tongue,

Lest you aren't thought vulnerable, your secrets are hung.

Yet when the guard is let down, the stew is spied upon,

Rotting with poison, rotting with all things evil, a villain
will be born.

Let it whistle, let it be treated, be disposed and destroyed,

Against skirmishes by it's sadist owner, whose feelings
have been toyed.

Yet when the fumes have been released, they reveal an ugly,
tortured spirit,

Howling in agony, contradicting it's peaceful mask,
yet finally freed.

Liberated from shackles of hiding, of concealing true nature,

Let the whistle blow, don't care about your stature.

Ice Cream Truck

What a reputation have you made for yourself, dear truck,

Treated as a coveted gem, or simply as muck.

The seller is a fairy, an angel of pleasure,
or ghastly Pennywise,

Ringing bells of temptation, to lure fresh meat,
as the suspenseful score does rice.

The Elixir of Life is sold, for which each price too less,

Or a disgusting excuse of nourishment, for which each
penny goes to waste,

Sore are opinions sitting on the extremes,
refusing to budge,

Injured "honour", injured ego rendering lame,
while the pain but only surge.

When, in fact, a cold, sweet article is sold by
a part time student,

A worker intending no harm, or magical ramblings,
to know so is more prudent.

The truck is neither a hearse, nor The Chariot Of God,

It's just a ten year old ice cream truck, business is all it
sought.

Ruin

Pillars weakening and falling apart,

Ceilings disintegrating, sceptres melting, a sight quite tart,

Or quite sweet, depends on who you are,

Yet a new edifice is coming up, not very far.

That shall fall, and crush all those inside it,

One may either observe with a smile, cherish, or seethe,

Or sob with sorrow, seeing it's destruction,

Only to repeat the same, by different parties, loss and gain
of pointless successions.

What dust, what ruin, surroundings worthy only of swine,

Yet this fate is tied, by destiny's twine,

The natural order of the universe, or simply events with
a common pattern, whatever you wish,

Yet everything is fine, still in flourish

Why I said "Never Again"

Trapped in a grove of Hemlock, no Wordsworth in
sight to rescue,

Till as far as nostalgic eyes could see, they were
the only view.

Though the innocent yet miserable suffering in
snow were visible too,

In a very selfish way, chose not to notice,
instead nurture own's cause of trickling dew.

From the eyes, which wish it didn't see the disgusting
sight,

Maybe cold calculations, lifeless warnings of logic are right,

Maybe it is not only naive to presume this time it would
change,

For now, the merry and caring enough is now miserable,
dyslexic, and even strange.

Spending the days wallowing in melancholic, rather
disgusting despair,

A peaceful mind in suicidal conflict, a soft idiotic soul in
downfall, reduced to a thing beyond repair.

The essence, the aura of anyone, so suddenly slain,

That's when I gave up hope, why I said "Never Again".

Your Thoughts

Between each giggle and rounds of merry making lie
a melancholic smile,

Reminiscing about you, and moments with you, as the
laughs can be heard from away a mile,

Though it is still easy to turn a deaf ear to cheer,

Longing for you has turned this holiday miserable, I fear.

Yet it's not your fault, for it lies with only me,

Everywhere I go, or rather escape, time spent
with you is all I feel and see,

Words traded are all that I really hear,

This longing is too cruel, too hard to bear.

Your thoughts are all that I think of when I'm away,

You can take advantage of me, and I will happily sway,

Your company is all I yearn, and to return is all I hope,

Your thoughts pull me back like a hostile rope.

Death

We are here, to mourn the loss, of a very good friend,

We are here, to mourn the loss, of sanity and intellect,
to perceive a fiend,

As it's very antonym, it's twin, rhyming word,

We are here, to mourn the loss, of the ability to hear our
own cries of help, barely heard.

We are here, to mourn the loss, of innocence of the sweet,
bright past,

Devoured by the Styx, a dark, dark present,
gulping the last,

Of any fragments left of a good time,

The crystal clear signs of a new age swiftly chime.

We mourn the loss of courage, the loss of a spine,

To admit, to even attempt to gulp down the pity in which
we wallow in, to say "all will be fine",

To not even try to make such a possible statement a truth,
we mourn the loss of faith,

A painful, agonizing, yet if acted upon,
only a potential death.